# LIGHT & SHADOW

*Poems*

SARA DEACON

*for Rob*

# CONTENTS

# Introduction

A lifetime ago, I was a ravenous student of poetry. I went to college and graduate school with aspirations of getting into the publishing industry while making a name for myself as a writer—specifically, as a poet. I hosted writing workshops at my apartment. I joined editorial teams of university literary magazines. I reveled in the beauty of language as I played and played with words.

The poems collected here were written during my time in graduate school (2003-2007). During those years, I also got married, bought a home and got pregnant with my first son.

I remember writing in my application essay for graduate school that no matter what path my education took, I expected to write poetry for the rest of my life. I was wrong.

Somewhere along the way, the poet in me went undercover. Verse became an afterthought—where it used to flow as naturally as breathing.

As I've learned over and over again in the twenty-plus years since my university days, life doesn't always play out the way we plan. So, as my attention turned to raising babies and making a home and a life for my family, the poems of my youth tucked themselves away in the dark, gathering dust.

Now, in midlife, I find myself drawn again to poetry. The landscape of language has changed dramatically over the intervening years, and the line that separates a poem from a meme is frightfully thin. As a student of visual poetry, I've often thought about how closely the two are related. The difference is subtle. A bath versus a shower. The former is luxurious—it requires intention, a certain level of focus and planning. The latter is efficient—it gets the job done, and you don't have to think about it too much. Both will get you clean. Only one invites you to float.

Now, I never abandoned writing entirely. I have written abundantly over the years—blogs, journals, social media content and website copy. Speeches and elevator pitches. Even though I haven't written as many poems as I had originally intended in the last couple of decades, my ecstasy over the written and spoken word has never waned. In fact, as an entrepreneur, I get to play with words now more than ever. As an emcee and speaker, my appreciation of vocal expression has deepened. As a publisher and author, I have been enriched by the written words of others as well as my own.

This collection of poems has been waiting almost twenty years to see the light—outside of the George Mason University library, that is, which is where I was told all of the graduate theses live. Written through times of extreme transition in the life of a twenty-something student during the early years of the current millennium, some of this content might seem tone-deaf or uncomfortable. I want to acknowledge that possibility while admitting that omission of the potentially offending lines didn't feel quite right, either. Most of these poems have their "I" wearing the skin of a fictional character—from a fairytale, from a nearly forgotten story, from a work of art. That's where they play—where I, myself, was playing at the time. Leaving them as is feels the most honoring, the most honest.

Poetry and art are meant to confront. To demand thought, attention, time. If you don't want to sit in that discomfort, turn the page. They're only words. From long ago and far away.

These days, I'm more comfortable on stage or writing nonfiction business books. And at the same time, I'm taking steps to heal and welcome back the poet underneath—she's done hiding and ready to play again.

— Sara NM Deacon, 2026

# MOMENTS

# Invitation

Lacking water,
love withers in
a matter of days.
As master of this body's
blemish, I choose
to reveal all,
my scroll unrolling.
Your choice:
to skim or to dive.

# LOVE POEM

stand                  make me
on a hill              beautiful

to speak my name       make me
say
in moderation
I love you
smiling                beautiful
imperfections
give height            enunciation
your voice
subtle enough
my name                yours

# A Girl Should be a Veil

But I am opaque
dancing in red—
a torn skirt
scuffed slippers tapping
trailing threads
passed to me from mothers.
It is July and the sun ignites
my shirt as I twirl
and run in purple flowers,
imaginary jewels.
My danger is heat
and light, spells and stories
hidden in hems
that bleed.

# Affair with the Evil Twin

8

Come,
  and bring your beard
to bed.
  I want to feel it
crunch
  between my teeth again.

# Just Another Day at the Office

She takes her shirt off in the dark.
She slides her shorts down in the dark.
The camera flashes.
She blinks her lashes.

Standing in the doorway, watching,
he shifts from foot to foot, watching.
His darkened silhouette
Lights a cigarette.

The camera blinks again.
She turns from it and him again.
He calls her beautiful.
She sighs, "How dull."

# Contract

She must learn
to sit next
hunger      and bathe
in its pale
fluorescent hum.
She must practice
restraint,
allow far
less chocolaty
nougat to break
the boundary
of her lips      (or none)—
take forty minutes
to bike, jog,
crunch stomach,
flatten daily
anxieties, smooth
obliques, skin.
She must remember
consequences
of temptation—
bulge wobble,
pinched inch,   distend—
must anticipate
rustle, rub
of loosening
clothes twirling

around tightening
waist.
She must          untrust
the mirror, trust
instead the ache
of adductors,
trust numbers—
tape measure,
circumference
of bicep,
collar-        bone's jut.
She must chew
more for familiar
pleasure
of mastication,
less for taste
or swallowing.
Focus
   on  drum  heads,
stretched
canvass, clasp
hands with want,
revel in empty
—the thrumming
space          within. She
must contract;
she must     begin.

# HUNGER

There's a jogger. And a dog on a leash. A retriever in a dirty brown coat. The jogger wears red shorts, white t-shirt hanging like a towel from the waistband. His shoulders are brown and glossy in the daylight. He doesn't wear a cap or sunglasses. My sunglasses are on the shelf. They continue down the street away from my building. The squares of light on the floor have spread into rectangles. There are different people with laptops and lattés at the café tables across the street. I am hungry. There's an old woman in a brown hat. She leans on a cane, walks short distances. Pauses. Walks some more. In the refrigerator, the milk has curdled. A crowd of kids in denim and sneakers rounds a corner, noisy cluster of cells moving down the street. Two carry basketballs in varying degrees of burnt orange or brown. I am hungry. The bread in the cupboard is already green. Spaghetti noodle boxes, cereal boxes, empty. The lettuce is brown in the fridge. There's a burst from a bicycle bell. It runs a red light at the intersection outside. The rider, in a yellow helmet, shines. Holds up a finger in the face of oncoming cross traffic. I fill a glass from the tap and drink.

# MICHELLE

I cannot trust that curve of hip, twist
of torso, face turned away and lost
to the shadows. But her shape still
holds my eyes like an old

photograph. That perfect arc from
ass to waist wants nothing I have
to offer. I'm close enough to
smell her, touch her savory skin, but

won't. I can't creep up on her, moon-
drenched and oblivious, can't stop
staring, tracing gazes over her cool
shoulder, along her quiet slide of spine.

# The Softness of Ragged Whiskers

I wasn't tired enough to sleep and rested
my head on his shoulder, hand near his cheek, I
stroked his beard with absentminded fingers and
thought of my dad while I stroked his beard, wondered
if I used to stroke his beard when my hands could
get lost in a beard's coarse hair, and what if that was my
beard, and how would it feel to have someone's hands
dancing though the hair of my beard, like mine wandered
through his beard, fingers testing texture, rolling hair
between them, more than a surface stroke of the beard, I found
comfort in the softness of ragged whiskers, like a child
clinging to familiar beard because these beards
are the beards that have kept me safe and will always.

# THE WAIT

After we offered up
our whole hand
our best attempt
face up on the table
for him to take (I
whispered, prayed
please take) or leave,
the phone sat silent,
and even when it
made some noise,
and my breath
paused, and my pulse
paused, it gave all
the wrong voices, gave
no news the rest of
the afternoon, the rest
of the whole day.

# OPAQUE

There you are,
pane of glass, roads
trees, houses all visible
beyond you.

I have everything
in sight & just because
I can see through you
doesn't mean it's easy.

Transparent still
divides, reveals a world
untouchable, dangles
possibles & prevents the reach.

# Cupid

17

perfume punctures
      bullet-hole, powder


ignition, explode—
      burns, burns, burns


—recovery will leave
      scars         scars

# SHE JUMPS

out windows, in
expensive clothes, gets
muddy, gets wet, breaks

      bones. Does it again. The
      first time, an accident, glass
      so clear the bird didn't know

            it was closed. She jumped
            in fear, tripped, got glass
            in her hair —    longer then,

                  tangled. Now, she jumps
                  on purpose, looks for new
                  windows, buys clothes—

                        cashmere or silk—boots to
                        match. Keeps crutches in
                        the closet, keeps windows

                            open.

# Unsigned Postcard

~~I was in love with you and I was~~
~~eight years old.~~ I was in love
with you and you thought

I was eight years old. True,
I wore saddle shoes and bows
in my hair. True, you had to shave

daily, your arms and chest
scattered with dark hairs.
You couldn't afford to be caught

looking at me the way I ~~wanted,~~
sometimes caught you looking.
I was a wandering orphan

who never asked for a father,
but you held onto my cursed little
hand ~~as I led you across the road.~~

I will always remember you
in doorways. And I will always
love you the way eight-year-olds

haven't thought of yet. Though
you never believed I was older
~~than I looked.~~ I carry the memory

of your chaste and fatherly kiss
in my pocket. I am still on the road,
wondering ~~who you walk with now,~~

if our paths will cross again—if
you would recognize me ~~without~~
~~all the sugar and spice.~~

PART 2

# ART

# Morning in the Forbidden City



Her sleeves will not silk
by me again, so silent
they lie as dust
blankets the yard to
muted jade.

In my rooms, I heavy
my single touch
echoed cold fallen nothing
leaves dry drifts, drifting
restfulness—where, away.

No peace, now no
peace, troubled
blood, silk of my body
ever trembling silk.

# Imperial Garden

Bright azalea—

> So many colors come and go from my sight
> each day, I could never recall every contrasting shade.

> Her tone lingered, like the impression of light
> as you blink, but clearer and more permanent.

Fragrant peony—

> The ant on the blossom, I navigated her contours.
> I remember in the hours before dawn, my nose

> at her nape, breathing the nectar of her hair.
> Her petals will not unfold for me again.

Sacred lotus beauty—

> Opens, revealing neat pistil...exposes me,
> red as flame. My body drew power from her

> spirit, sweet and warm, as hers drew mine.
> Her voice was soft as whispered prayers.

Delicate wintersweet—

> And the air grows warmer, and the blooms
> wither, and I cannot bear watching them
>
> lose their seats to the uniform green leaves.
> There will be other flowers—how will I see them?

# TO PAINT A PICTURE IS EITHER VERY SIMPLE OR IMPOSSIBLE

Split open

Viscera

Elbowdeep    more

Sure    Reality

Sharpened    soft

On a crutch

# My Lonesome Cowboy

*after Takashi Murakami*

Brightly painted blue hair and peach skin
in cartoon stance, wide legged and naked,
the cowboy has taken hold of himself,
hand and prick guiding the lasso of cream
a thick spiral reaching above his head,
his arm extended in show and tell
gesture. He does not sit, bent awkwardly
in a corner on the floor by himself,
hidden in his knees, hand cupping a sad
drip. He can't conceal what comes naturally.
You can be yourself.

# TRIANGLE

*inspired by an Elliot Erwitt photograph*

Filled with light and shadow
a bedroom kept by tattered
walls, a bed, the regal shape
of feline gazing at infant there
naked, facing mother. Light
glancing over baby's back and
mother's hair and forehead.
The sheets are rumpled.
The cat contemplates
what cats contemplate
when mother brings another
home, when suddenly this new
thing has the lion's share
of she who leans enraptured
cheek upon her hand upon
the mattress, her gaze so
filled with light and shadow.

# Essential Study

The same show of cruelty is essential: fingers
bent toward folded hands, poems and related sciences
possessed at the moment she is folded
like a piece of cloth possessed
every three days, desire is darkened.

The moment should be studied
in red flowers, the art and care of the body,
the poems, red flowers of the body
imitating, it appears, against purpose.

It is possible to embrace right
to the end.

He has ejaculated sincere feelings, his life
spread purely in fire. Purely by chance, words develop
desire. Words develop fire. He traces

three or four lines on her shoulder, on her breasts,
her thighs, her red flowers, with the nail of his thumb.
She will know meaning in folded forms between.

# Utamaro Object

A flattened message, tossed in the corner
and forgotten at his feet, doesn't line up parallel
with the black cube where the mirror reflects her curling toes.

On the other side, against the wall, her hair
has tumbled in lines more precise than the scribbled
words obscured where paper folds haphazardly in on itself.

This must have been good news, or else
why the celebration, the promise of primal thrust?
Or a message too nuanced to trust to ink and paper —

best delivered in the flesh.

# Untitled

*based on the painting "Street in Venice" by John Singer Sargent*

No one calls her name tonight,
      even if they know it, or remember,
and she knows not five minutes from now,
the same men who pause their conversation
      to notice the swirl of her skirt, her clicking
      heels on stone, the flower in her hair
will turn back to each other, slipping
again into the cadence of their banter without
another thought to where she's come from,
where she's walking, or what shouted syllables
      might make her turn her head.

# Ophelia

Wildflowers in her hair, red
and white ones, their subtle stems in green.
Wildflowers clutched in her hand,
the same hand clutching the skirt of her blue
dress, trimmed in gold, a hem
that curves to lift, reveals the red
under-skirt where one foot steps forward
over grass beneath. Her pale
hand rests on a knot on the trunk of a multi-brown
shaded tree. The grass is long, painted
in highlights and shadows with flat-leaved
plants contributing to the greens.

Her hair, reflecting the hues of tree bark,
hints a little toward red—the flowers,
her own plump unsmiling lips, the blush
on her cheek and round her vague staring eyes.

Behind her, a pond or slow creek, dark blue-gray
with lily pads floating, a muted green.
Behind her, a wooden bridge in straight strokes.
Behind her, shade from another tree, sitting darkly
near the bank. Behind her, on the bridge,
two children, or nymphs, observing.

# Painted

Imagine colors. I can make your
face sing. Long after you are gone
and I, flung out into remnants,
the image remains. After burning
into black and white—you become
a ghost transparent, done up
done in satisfying sky, blue hand
undone.

There is a deceptive innocence to
your staring image. I obfuscate you
quietly, secluded in my undertones.
I panic your flesh tones, that
you discover my child's game beneath
keeps no secrets. This, your face
and those, his hands. I am yellow.
You are.

I could not have shaped and snapped
this shot without your sleeping. I could
not have pinned colors to skin
without him. I could have been
crimson or indigo, too. This is no
tongueless fiction. Now you realize
his eyes have been blazing this
whole time.

Washes. My tiny brushes wash
artifice off eyelids, wash skin
from butterfly mouths. Wash you
into bluish mist. Wash myself out
of the picture. Wash men into alien
articles of themselves. Wash ancestry
into black background hues. Watch me
make belief.

# Reflections

*based on the painting "Mother and Child" (c.1905) by Mary Cassatt*

She's old enough to know
her own blue eyes and soft
blond hair, old enough to
see their similarity to the woman
in flowing gold who holds up
the little mirror for her peering.

She's old enough to mimic
percussions of speech, to twist
her small pink mouth into other
shapes and experiment with
volume. She's aware that her gaze
is not alone, resting on those lips.

She's old enough to know this
lap connects to Mother, this chair
gives shelter with creaking green
rhythms, and the hand on her
bare shoulder translates loosely
into love, keeps her from tipping.

But she doesn't know why
Mother turns away from her
own reflected face, to focus on
her daughter's naked beauty,

why every look must be noted,
or how much she's already grown.

# Beauty and the Violin

How's this for a fairy tale:

> Beautiful, Young, Blonde,
> a Princess to boot
> captures the heart of a lonely prince-type.
>
> He leads her off to a humble cottage
> somewhere in the middle of nowhere
> or the woods. She coyly follows.
>
> And they live...

But that's not quite how this one goes.

> Before the princess could walk
> she knew that in beauty lies power.
> And she knew she was beautiful beyond
>
> measure. So as soon as her hair glimmered
> in the sun, she had her pick of princely suitors.
> And before her puberty was over,
>
> she had left many men weeping in her wake.
> This one was only different
> because he played violin and had a temper
>
> her coyness couldn't calm.

How's that for a fairy tale?

>     Beauty, Torn Tresses, Dirty Apple Cheeks.
>     Afraid to speak above a whisper,
>     she only longs for sleep.

PART 3
# GENERATION

# Juniper Tree



Branches twine
a twisting reach,
whisper of needles
trembling, another wish
fed blood to dry
earth, and we wait
long for fruit.

# Matins

Sunday morning
       no space between skin
he breathes
       from the top of his throat
       beside me.
My fingers float
       along my abdomen, my
       eyes sealed to swelling light
       linger in dissipating
       dream.
A hollow rumble
       and he rolls his weight
       slides an arm around
       me, my middle—he
slips
       his hand beneath
my hand there
       and pulls me into him.
       Our palms—open—press
       empty.

# MORULA

Three days after fertilization—conception,
eight large cells cluster and float
through translucence, my interior twilight,

towards home. Already, you have a name,
unwhispered. Already you have gone
from one to eight through the miracle

of biology. Invisible cluster, soon multiplied
to millions, billions, more—but I can't
think of you in those larger numbers yet,

the vast uncertainties of your future:
nerves, bones that grow, a mind and eyes
of your own, fingers, toes, a beating heart...

Today I only count to three or eight, and pause
a moment there to let you be the blackberry—
*morula*—in eight sections I can't yet feel

with any of my many trillion cells. Though,
by now, you have probably moved on
to sixteen, or thirty-two, I am not quite there.

# SURRENDER

Let the sparrow hop and snowflakes
        drop and soak the roads.
Let cars and drivers go too fast.


Let a woman open her umbrella
        in a faint drizzle.
Let her crisp heels click like time.


Let the man read his newspapers,
        sip his triple espresso.
Let him furrow his brow, tap his foot.


Let someone's pockets empty,
        let someone else's overflow.
Let wars continue, end, begin.


Let weeks run by in headlines
        of disease, scandal, shame.
Let the sun melt ice, soothe breezes.


Let one moment pass, and then
        another. Let each cell rush,
divide, revise or take its time—

let go—surrender to gravity, let galaxies,
          moons, and atoms spin—
your fears have no control.

# Five Kinds

I forgot to mention the five kinds of kisses:
       1. a watercolor wash
       2. a saturated color print
       3. sticky acrylic (practiced in the best society)
       4. charcoal / pencil blends
       5. drybrush
"Three kinds are suitable for love affairs."


I meant to mention such forms of
       spilled color spread in water, evaporating—
       red flowers printed in black&white—
       sticking the wrong surface—
       charcoal smudged (besides the places indicated)—
       eager brushes—
and "any inconveniences this may have."


The "vulnerable part" was this:
       to brutally mention inconveniences (so much
       red powder that the day is darkened). I
       mention inconveniences, "use red flowers"
       to draw three kinds of kisses.
       I forgot their names.
He traces these unmentionable kisses. I name them.

# Inheritance

> I form my rhythm      before knowing air
>      your voice    and breath
> dance in languid opposition      to my rapid pulse
>      introduce      staccato, crescendo
>      sarcastic rise
> and fractured fall      to the darkness
>      of your body
> touch the vernix      on these new ears
>
> without grammar
>      or      vocabulary
>      I learn      poetry
> grasp at slim variations      in light
>      I float      on your tones
>      suck a lullaby
>      from my      thumb
>
> Mother, you
>      teach me language
> your melismas in my blood
> before my voice      emerges
>      more than reflex
> this cadence      when
>      I finally cry      my breath
>      I know you
> in the patterns
>      of my own displaced      wailing
>      return to you
> with every      squawk and song

# QUICKENING

Even knowing how a goldfish
life is short,

I gave it a name as it wiggled around
all undulating gills, rippling fins

and searching mouth in its temporary
plastic baggie home. I cupped it

in my hands, feeling the fish nudge
my palms through the thin membrane—

my mother compared the flutter to a child
finding its way around the womb.

When I wake up to feel you poking
around the temporary home of my body,

I might find a better metaphor, learning
more about miracles, and

I will begin to name you, noting
how quickly time's already floated by.

# Mommy, Draw Me

Here is a pencil, and paper to color on
because paper is where we draw,
not walls and not arms or table surfaces.

Today I want to know this letter,
it sounds in my name, and its name
sounds like "em—" draw me an M.

Some straight lines connect to each
other on top, leaning but balanced,
not what I expected. Now let me try.

Here is a crayon because I think that
letter "ay" should be green, get your
paper and draw me A. Now my turn.

Here is my paper flowing with A's, with
M's. I do how you show me, how I ask and
now begin writing with, "am...am...am..."

# Of Tissue and Language

First, contact—abrupt, unexpected.

Then, a faint pink rise in the flesh,

> tenderness,
> numbness,
> tenderness, sting.

Watch it change colors
        before your very eyes:

> pale
> bluish
> greenish
> spidery purple.

Iced down,
        the pace of its change will slow
        to stop the swelling or splitting of skin,
        the temperature of it all will drop significantly.


After that, the skin will darken,
the spidery purple dappled maroon
begins to radiate noticeable heat.

Press your fingers to it—


      feel a twinge
      pain working itself out
      through pain.


Evidence of force,


      physical or
      inspirational:
      muse or
      softball.


Poetry—the visible bruise—


      attracts the injured
      and the curious
      with its mechanics
      of tissue and language,
      of muscle and blood.

# ANATOMY

I have symmetrical bones,
starburst vertebrae,
twenty-seven bones in one hand
to match 27 in the other.

I have fibrous joints
and cartilaginous joints
and synovial joints,
like everyone else,

and too many muscles
in my head, in my back,
stomach and feet
to count. Muscles

working all day long
for the tibia, toiling
against the femur
or humerus, to walk

and reach. But my left
thumb bends both ways,
and my foot's phelange
is thin sliced, screwed tight.

My palmar interossei
can wrap around the knife
but can't keep the butter
balanced on it.

# MILESTONE OF CREATION



Considering origins,
        he drew himself up
as if to mumble
        the last words on the edge
of the last world.
        About the whole
lot of humans,
        words continue to fall,
the sentence
        ever ending in period.


Each experiment
        ends with a conclusion
not always anticipated
        in hypothesis—
the breathed Word
        that started everything,
created chaos, then
        wiped clean to begin again. If
he banished the Word,
        would it all end for good?

Having lived complete
        with words so long, it takes
some strength to un-
        remember names of things,
to dismantle and recalibrate
        the elements of thought.


As the last world faded
        into a background of stars,
he saw what he had destroyed,
        and it was

# Part 4
# Story

# THE HUNTER

My knife is sharp. It curves along
       the swollen belly
of the snoring wolf. The blood
       takes a moment
before revealing its bright red line,
       its grim smile.
Wriggling fingers find the incision
       then a hand, arm.
I reach to her reaching, the blood
       wells up, the smell
pricks my nostrils. My knife falls,
       my hands pull flesh
apart, revealing her soaking cap,
       her matted curls.
Her face turns toward me,
       like I've found her
secret hiding place, spoiled a game
       she wants to play
again. I lift her body gently.
       She squirms out
of my grasp, and goes to work
       pushing innards
aside to rouse the grandmother,
       who takes longer
to wake. And when she wakes,
       she notices
tears in her nightgown, reaches
       for a garment

to cover her shame. I hand her
        the wolf's blanket,
the blanket from her own bed,
        most of it unsoiled.
It is not my idea to fill the animal
        up with stones,
to torture before the kill—after all,
        it was only instinct—
I turn from Grandmother, and find
        Red returning
from outside, two large stones
        weighing down
her two skinny arms, skin dotted
        with drying blood.
"They're from the garden," she says,
        "Grandmother
won't mind." She drops them
        on the bed, can't
reach the open body without climbing,
        and she runs back
outside for more. I place each one
        deep in the stomach.
They clack together. I close the wound.
        With the last stitch,
the snoring stops, the wolf sits up,
        sees me, the girl,
the old woman, and strains to run.
        I look at my hands
large and rough, bloodstained
        from more than this.
I do not see, but I hear the groan
        and final thud.

# The Stepsister's Silence

*"What should we give her for being so naughty and having such a wicked and greedy heart that makes her so stingy?"*
*"Each time she utters a word, a toad shall spring out of her mouth. This will be my gift."*

Alone
in the kitchen, I might
say a few words while I
lean over the boiling
water.

I have
learned how to prepare the
creatures that leap from my lips
with each syllable so
that my

cuisine
has become known throughout
the land.

Outside
of my kitchen, no one
has heard my voice in years—
so many now that I've
lost count.

I have
never been beautiful.

I have never been kind
or good.

At least
with silence, I remain
a bit mysterious.
The silence offers some
solace.

I have
tried to make the best of
this affliction, sustained
myself with brief whispers
and the rhythms of my
lonesome

life. There
are bad days, of course. And
times when I think I should
venture back into the
forest,

attempt
to show how I have grown,
reformed, and accepted
my fate,

at least
attempted thoughtfulness.
Would this be enough to
reverse or lighten this
foul curse?

I am
afraid not. That girl I
was still lives in this skin
somewhere.

I feel
her squirming, and raging

under my flesh. She still
feels that if there must be
toads, they should at least have
gold bones.

As much
as I have grown, I know
it will not be enough.
I can never open
my mouth

expect
an aria to fan
out and enchant the world.
Instead,

I will
feed folk with my whispered
words, drop them in with a
splash and a hiss. I will
accept

their praise
of my unique cuisine,
keep the words consumed a
secret locked behind shut-
up lips.

# More Than a Wish



It was more than a wish
that made you.


And more than blood
on a blanket of snow
or window frame's dark gleam
brought the idea
of you to my heart.


Red as blood.
White as snow.
Black as ebony.

Incantation, mantra
only words pulsing
bodies to body,
blood to birth.


My girl body
was not strong enough
to split us.

Black ebony night.
Blood slicked red.
Still white snow.


Your story
        will always begin
        with a wish, pulse,
        push and blood:


a glossy broken
        *once upon a time.*

# FAIR

Mirror, mirror on the wall
all I ever wanted was to like
the look of my dark reflection.
Even back when you assured
me I was fairest, something
rang false in my opinion.

Beneath my crown, my ears
appeared uneven and my eyes
seemed two unmatched shades.
Age brought lines to indicate
some years of frowning and
hands' skin paled to blue veins.

When you called my stepdaughter
fairer, for the first time I believed
your simple proclamations
in admiration of the beauty
I so desired and yet possessed,
oblivious to my own fair reflection.

# Gifts for Snow White

*"Beware of your stepmother," they said.*

I. The Staylace

With silken cords she laced me so gently up
to the final pull, and smiled
at my beauty, gone breathless.

II. The Comb

In the tiny tarnished mirror
I watched her solemnly
lift my tresses, comb poised in her fingers.

III. The Apple

Inviting as myth, big and supple and red. My lips
part at her request. I
wonder, how many deaths will please her?

# SNOW WHITE LIVES

66

Don't tell her
I found her
more enticing
under glass.

# Rapunzel in Exile

1.

She bruised my arm when she dragged me deeper
into the thick of the trees.
She was so much stronger
than those crooked old fingers might suggest.

When she tossed me to the ground, she turned
as if to begin her journey back
to the tower or another place.
But she lingered, and began to speak.

I almost couldn't hear the words over the rustle
of leaves and the chirping birds,
and I was so heavy.
But I realized she had begun to tell a tale.

*Once upon a time, I lived next door to a thief.*
*I made a deal... She made a promise...*
*She gave me a daughter.*
*I let her have her fill.*

*I should have let her keep you.*

And by the time I turned my face toward her
voice, she had gone.
I remained prostrate
in the dirt until nightfall. Through to morning.

2.

Confronted with only two options--to live
or to die--I chose the more difficult.

3.

I thought often of the prince,
his sweet words, the comfort
of his body, his skin and mine.
I knew what we had done.
She let me know well what we had done.

I didn't expect those waves of pain,
but they did not surprise me.
What surprised me
was what my body knew,
even with all of the screaming.

4.

I cried with them as they came into the world,
and I didn't stop when they settled into the crooks of my arms, into
sleep.
And I didn't stop when they woke and wailed again,
or when I held their open mouths against my aching breasts.

For so long our sobs were interchangeable.
And it rained so hard over us, those first few days.
I didn't know if it would ever stop.
I don't know if it ever did.

# A Moment of Light

My babies are asleep
        snug in petticoat pillows, smelling of pine.
The girl kicks her tiny legs
        and curls, then stretches out her toes.
She trusts the air around her
        mingling with my breath.
The boy sucks his small fist
        a slick of saliva shines on his knuckles
and he hums
        a milk-satisfied song.


I remember
        how they swam together inside me,
        how I forgot–for a moment–the tower, the witch-
        mother, the prince...
I remember
        a story of rapunzel, a mother's craving,
        how she gave her daughter over to the spells of witches,
        heights, and men...


In this wilderness


I could wish for stone walls and a roof
        to replace these sticks and leaves,
        which do little to keep the rain out;

I could wish for bread and wine, a certain fragrant vegetable,
        or cheese and sauces flavored with
        spices whose names I can't pronounce;
I could wish for a warm bath, a proper haircut,
        a new dress, a good book to lean my daydreams on;
I could wish for a mother, a prince, a savior.


        All those wishes have high prices.
        Those cravings lead to promises
        that can never be reversed or broken.


The girl blinks
        and rests her gaze on my face.
The boy grunts
        and smiles in his simple dream.
The sunlight
        touches us through the leaves.


This is the wish
        I never thought to wish before.
And now, all I can think to wish
        is this.

# PRINCELING

She tells me stories that start with, "Once upon a time..."
and gives the animals voices like our own.
        Thoughts and wishes, too.


She uses words like, *king* and *witch* and *father* and I think
these must be very powerful animals,
        more so even than wolves.


When she sings—always the same song—her words melt together
and they're hard to understand sometimes.
        I think I heard *tower* once, and *hair*.


I don't think I ever asked what a *castle* or a *slipper* was,
but I think that *gold* and *glass* must be valuable objects
        that help people live happily.


She calls me her *princeling*, and I wonder
if that is another made-up word. Because in her stories,
        *princes* live in *castles*.


Not in huts made of branches with floors made of dirt.
Not in the wilderness where all the courtiers are trees.
        And their fathers are kings.

# Rapunzel's Daughter and the Garden

Watching someone coax life from bland dirt is different than doing it yourself. Mother was never very good at raking, planting, knowing how the sprout will take root, and where it will thrive. She seems like a character in some of her own stories, a princess who has everything provided. I think she did a lot of watching in her life.

But I was churning the earth before I could walk. With sticks, my toes, my ragged fingernails. I always knew where to dig. Mother never had to show me. Before we were born to her, she learned some of the forest's tricks. What berries burned on her tongue, what leaves made her sweat and sick in the grass.

My brother likes to wander, most of the time. But in the evenings, mother sings and braids rope, and we sit together in my garden.

I asked my mother what is the name of each leafy thing? She told me that if I name them myself, I will never go hungry. So I whisper their names, *brakel*, *farngen*, *sveary*, *tilk*, and it seems right to me.

Mother says she is named for a vegetable. For a craving Mother's mother had once upon a time. I think it would be easy to love a vegetable that much. I sit in my garden and breathe deeply. I call the most fragrant plant the same name my mother calls me.

# FISH

Once, I rippled just below the surface, where only blue sunlight could
see; I ate seaweed, small fish with the scales on.
I had an iridescent smile; when I left the water, it was for you I learned
to cook root vegetables, rice with sea salt and ground pepper,
chops of meat.
You tell me I swim strange, in the pool in summer; I no longer have a
secret coral life.
You used to sit in the bathtub for hours, not even reading, just
watching your fingertips shrivel and your palms go soft; there
was a memory.
I used to distill oxygen with parts of my body I do not remember:
before I was polluted with soap.
You say the world is beautiful; I remember it bluer, blurry and floating.
You think that the reason I do not wear high-heeled shoes is a
bone defect in my feet; the truth is that walking on land is
treacherous enough without unnecessary heights.
I would rather swim long distances—my rhythmic muscles clench,
unclench, propel; we are no longer underneath.
Once, there was no such thing as dancing, and I never missed it because
of natural rippling, muffled sun, light on water, on the scales
of our tails.
When I hear wind chimes, the tapping of harpsichords, oboes, I think
of blue, deepening; I remember you, dancing in waves.
I remember the world is beautiful, differently.

# THE ORGAN ROOM

74

The keys and buttons, levers, switches line
internal sphere, suspended center-point.
A chandelier made out of chandeliers
illuminates this random room in red.

The giant clock is standing keeping time—
but which exactly? Who are we to judge
the spiral stairs and beer steins on the wall?

There's nothing silent here. A symphony
of discord runs the halls; the organ plays
itself—but only if you ask it twice.

# THE KING'S BUFFET

She contemplates a portion of salad. Radicchio, arugula, spinach leaf, a cucumber slice, grape tomato, a few shreds of carrot she has drizzled with a thin Italian dressing. She pierces the skin of the tomato with the tines of her fork and anticipates the sweetness of its juice.

She considers a forkful of rice. The grains are long, mixed white and dark, dark brown. She chews. She tastes. She remembers pouring gravy, a lingering glance.

She handles chicken roughly, pushing it around in its juices, sawing it with a knife, speculating about the spices in the marinade and his wife. The tender flesh yields easily between her teeth. With each flex of her jaw, with each swallow, she becomes more involved.

She separates the onions from the rest of the mixed vegetables with deliberate dignity, that is, without using her fingers more than absolutely necessary, listening for his voice through the clink of utensil and glass. The bread plate is useful for holding these unwanted things. She eats each piece of overdone yellow squash and zucchini, knowing no amount of salt or pepper can save them from their blandness.

She acknowledges the banana cream pie. She approaches a section one
quarter the area of the sweet circle, more than she should
allow. She selects a more modest slice to lose herself in. She
lets it melt off the fork and onto her tongue, disappearing bite
after bite.


She sips her coffee stirred with sugar and would fill her plate again if
no one was watching.

# THE FIDEAL

I ended up on rocks, water
clicking tongues near my shoes.
I was alone. Thinking. Alone, I
was not scared of the dark.

Until the singing
came sailing over the lake
through trees, made me
uneasy. That low

longing call to me.
I edged around the bank,
scuffed stones into wet
crevasses between, trying

to distance myself, but
instead, carried closer to this
knife of a voice, thought
abandoned me. I shivered

when cool lips touched
my lips with the brown tang
of earth and a voice still
singing and lips kissed

and kissed, drawing me
into the scatter of night. Cold
arms led me closer
to the water

I couldn't argue against.
I woke as arms let go, body
and lips all gone—one gasp
mouthful of water and

weeds.
The moon was a pin
of light, receding. Then
it was gone, too.

# About the Author



Sara Deacon is an award-winning speaker, professional emcee, publisher, coach and author of the book *Welcome to the Stage: The 360° Approach to Hosting Events Like a Pro*.

With advanced degrees in English and Creative Writing, her journey as a writer and editor gives her a storytelling edge, helping her craft narratives that resonate with a wide range of audiences, making her a driving force behind impactful events and publications alike.

When she's not holding a microphone or playing with words, Sara loves connecting deeply with people who are passionate about their own purpose. With Sara in the room, you'll rise to the next challenge, knowing you have a genuine cheerleader and supporter in your corner.

She lives in Milwaukee, Wisconsin with her husband and three sons.